The Little Black Book of Swagger

Book of Swagger

637 Swagger Tips for Super Achievers

ERNIE J. ZELINSKI

Visions International Publishing
P.O. Box 4072
Edmonton, Alberta, Canada, T6E 4S8
Phone: 780-434-9202   Email: vipbooks@telus.net

Distributed to Canadian bookstores by Sandhill Book Marketing, Unit #4 - 3308 Appaloosa Road, Kelowna, B.C., V1V 2W5 (info@sandhillbooks.com) and to US bookstores by National Book Network, 4501 Forbes Blvd., Ste. 200, Lanham, MD (Phone: 800-462-6420)

The Little Black Book of Swagger / Ernie J. Zelinski
ISBN 978-1-927452-09-7

Printed in Canada

Other Creative Works by Ernie J. Zelinski

The Lazy Person's Guide to Success (over 110,000 copies sold)

Look Ma, Life's Easy (published in 7 languages)

Life's Secret Handbook (limited leather edition only)

Career Success Without a Real Job (published in 5 languages)

The Lazy Person's Guide to Happiness (over 80,000 copies sold)

The Joy of Being Retired: 365 Reasons Why Retirement Rocks — and Work Sucks!

The Joy of Not Working (over 315,000 copies sold)

How to Retire Happy, Wild, and Free (over 460,000 copies sold)

The Book of Swagger (companion to *The Little Black Book of Swagger*)

About the Author

Ernie J. Zelinski is an international best-selling author, prosperity life coach, innovator, speaker, and unconventional career expert. Ernie's previous seventeen creative works — published in twenty-two languages in twenty-nine countries — have sold over 1,100,000 copies worldwide. One of Ernie's Swagger moves is driving a raunchy rusted-out 1995 Camry 2-dr. coupe even though he can purchase a brand new Lamborghini or two for cash. On the other hand, he practically always flies Business Class or International Business Class to places such as Honolulu, Prague, Istanbul, Toronto, New York, London, and Vancouver. He is known to have been invited by two pilots of a Dreamliner on two occasions to join them for a talk in the cockpit once the respective planes landed in Honolulu and Vancouver. Ernie has autographed three chairs (the hat trick) at the iconic Bistro Praha Restaurant in Edmonton whereas famous former Edmonton Oilers players such as Wayne Gretzky, Mark Messier, and Kevin Lowe have had the privilege of signing only one. Ernie is presently working on another remarkable book — as he always is.

Introduction

In modern society Swagger is entitled to no moral standing whatsoever and yet it sits in a place of honor at the tables of the proud and influential. Truth be known, many ordinary mortals fret about their lack of Swagger. At the same time, they envy those who have it — particularly many super achievers of this world. If you are one of these people who would like to exhibit genuine flair, this book may just help you in more ways than one.

If you rise to most occasions with complete fearlessness and unwavering confidence, you likely have Swagger. Unshakable confidence is certainly better than living in constant fear and anxiety, debilitated with depression. For all intents and purposes Swagger is the art of loving yourself as much as you love others, at the same time being grateful for being the person you are. How can that be bad? Super achievers are good at this.

What exactly is "Swagger"? Much like pornography, it's not easy to define. Let's just say it's an overflowing confidence that radiates from the person's being. The person embraces his or her own greatness even if others don't. It's a form of arrogance but Swagger is not a bad thing, as many people believe.

There is a lot of Swagger advice in this little book. Profundity abounds. This book may even painfully inoculate you with some harsh wisdom. You can take the Swagger advice and do whatever you want with it. Take it and run with it. Tell your friends about it. Whatever you do with it, you will find the most compelling advice about Swagger ever presented in a little book like this.

Swagger comes as a result of doing things in a certain way. Super achievers, who do things in a certain way, whether on purpose or accidentally, have Swagger. Those who do not do things in this way, no matter how hard they work at it or how able they are, remain swaggerless.

☙

There are three types of Swagger: Raunchy Swagger (RS), Elegant Swagger (ES), and Super Swagger (SS). Whatever the type, Swagger gives you intrigue, something the mediocre in society don't have.

☙

Swagger favors the bold.

If Swagger was easy, everyone would have it. Seldom has a person who lived an easy life left a name worth remembering.

ㆍ

Achievers with Swagger never take the path of least resistance simply because victory is not to be found on that path.

ㆍ

The first duty of super achievers is to create their own Swagger. That's how they differentiate themselves from others.

ㆍ

There was never Genius without at least a tint of Swagger.

ㆍ

The more new things you do and get good at, the more Swagger you will have.

You don't need to know where the path you have chosen will lead you exactly. Not knowing where you're going and traveling that path confidently and with flair is what gives you Swagger.

୧

Individuals with Swagger, like solitary trees, if they grow at all, grow strong, prosperous, and free.

୧

Swagger compels you not to escape your problems but to confront them courageously.

୧

Always go with the choice that scares you the most because that's the one which will help you develop more Swagger.

Some people claim Swagger is not a woman's thing. Not so! Jen Sincero has Swagger. Oprah has Swagger. The late Sharka Svajgr, co-owner of the Czech style Bistro Praha restaurant, had Swagger. Incidentally, Sharka's last name "Svajgr" in Czech is pronounced "Swagger". How cool is that! Sharka had double Swagger — with her last name and with her cool, confident behavior.

A ship is safe in the harbor but it has no Swagger. In the same vein, rough seas make for able sailors with Swagger.

❧

The question isn't who is going to let you display your Swagger; it's who is going to stop you?

❧

You cannot develop Swagger by avoiding life's problems.

❧

Swagger begins when you exit your comfort zone.

❧

Swagger is not following the path where it may lead; Swagger is going where there is no path and leaving one's own trail.

Individuals with Swagger would rather attempt something remarkable and fail than do something irrelevant and succeed.

ଜ

Swagger is the fuel in us that needs to be ignited with sparks of ingenuity and boldness.

ଜ

Winning may not provide everything to the character with Swagger, but losing provides far less.

ଜ

In the republic of mediocrity, Swagger is despised.

ଜ

Super achievers with Swagger never adopt another person's definition of success as their own.

Achievers with Swagger operate differently than the crowd. They have an eye for the things that are essential for attaining true success.

Practically anyone can develop as least some Swagger. Giving up on ever having Swagger because you believe that you can't develop it is definitely not a Swagger move.

The great creative individual is capable of more Swagger than a large group of ordinary people can ever muster.

Characters with Swagger will always encounter violent opposition from mundane, jealous minds.

What is Swagger but the power of expressing a much more powerful individuality?

❧

You don't need to be a genius or a sports hero or even a university graduate to have Swagger. You just need a framework built on competence and confidence.

❧

To have Swagger, you have to be original. If you're like everyone else, what's the point?

❧

Ill fortune never crushes an individual with Swagger.

❧

Financial Swagger is having a credit score higher than 850.

Even when an achiever with Swagger is in the gutter, he or she is still focusing his or her dreams toward the upper realms of the Universe.

਒

Swagger is to know your true self, to say what you want to say to others, and not to get too concerned if they are offended by hearing the truth.

਒

Lifestyle reporter Elizabeth Bernstein of the *Wall Street Journal* recently advised, "It's time to be your own life coach." That's what individuals with Swagger do. They don't hire a life coach. They are their own life coach, because they are their own best friends and take full responsibility for their own lives.

Swagger in itself is much more musical than any rap song.

Those who are different and have Swagger change the world for the better. Those who are ordinary and resent Swagger do their best to keep it the way it is.

Achievers with Swagger rarely give advice. They know that the individuals who need it most will most likely ignore it most.

Individuals with Swagger don't hate losers. They just feel much better when they aren't around them.

To super achievers with Swagger, moral victories don't count.

Leaders with Super Swagger listen to advice from the experts — and then spectacularly ignore it — as Ukrainian President Volodymyr Zelensky did proclaiming, "I don't need a ride. I need ammunition!"

The achiever with Swagger knows that the best way to get rid of the full-goose bozos of this world is to tell them something important that is for their own good.

There is no significant Swagger without a touch of madness.

When individuals with Swagger want to cheer up themselves, they do so by cheering up someone else.

An achiever with Swagger has his or her wits grow sharper by doing magical things that others are afraid of doing.

No one is prevented from having Swagger by lack of riches.

Individuals with Swagger never play the victim game. Famous American diplomat Condoleezza Rice couldn't have said it any better: "Never think of yourself as a victim. Because if you do, you have given control of your life to someone else." Of course, if you give your control of your life to others, they will have very little — likely nothing good — planned for you.

☙

If you have true Swagger, your courage will always rise to greater heights when someone attempts to belittle you.

☙

It's easy to live the expected and conventional. Achievers with Swagger know that it's when you live the unexpected and unconventional that you start having fun with your life.

Like Einstein, the individual with Swagger questions everything even if it represents generations of conventional wisdom.

☙

Equality is a lie. There will never be true equality — not in democratic countries, not in socialist countries, and not in any other forms of countries. Understanding this is central to being a person with Swagger.

☙

Nobody cares if you are miserable so you might as well show some Swagger when you are.

☙

Like happiness, Swagger can't be bought with money. But a bit of extra money may help you develop more of it.

You will have no true Swagger unless you can live bravely, excitedly, and imaginatively.

❧

You can start by showing some real Swagger by throwing all of your dreams into space and seeing what it will send back.

❧

Failing with Swagger is a subtle form of success.

❧

Achievers with Swagger never make stupid mistakes. They only make sensational, intelligent ones from which they learn a lot.

❧

Individuals with Swagger not only win but they also lose with Swagger — it's just another form of winning to them.

Swagger allows you to go and make interesting mistakes, even amazing mistakes, and even more importantly, glorious and fantastic mistakes.

✿

After a few spectacular failures, super achievers with Swagger are not satisfied with mere ordinary success.

✿

The great ideas that characters with Swagger generate are hammered out by themselves, and are not developed by others or with others.

✿

It's better to be despised because of one's Swagger than to be totally forgotten because of one's modesty and obscurity.

Swagger varies inversely with the number of boring friends a person hangs around with.

ᙏ

Achievers with Swagger don't succeed because they are destined to; they succeed because they are determined to.

ᙏ

Swagger is knowing that your worst shot was still damn good — and better than most people's best shots.

ᙏ

Once you've developed a certain measure of Swagger, you mustn't lose it. Build on it.

ᙏ

Swagger is not for the faint of heart.

Men and women with Swagger never fight battles with small-minded people. They have much bigger things to do with their lives.

When an achiever with true Swagger appears on the scene, you will know the person by this sign: All the mediocre minds will be in fierce opposition to him or her.

An achiever with Swagger will not talk to a media person who is hard up for material.

Super achievers with Swagger put out great work that is scarce. They certainly don't waste it on jerks, selfish hustlers, or those who won't appreciate it.

Individuals with Super Swagger do not ever apologize for their sensational success. Never! Why would they? This would be like a zebra apologizing for its spots or a Krispy Kreme doughnut apologizing for being super delicious.

∝

Achievers with Swagger don't play for safety — because they know that safety in itself can be the most dangerous thing in the world.

∝

Delusional people making comments on the Internet think they have solved a problem. The individual with Swagger has avoided the problem and the fools surrounding the problem altogether by not going on Facebook.

Swagger is the natural companion of Creativity.

❧

When you always find yourself on the side of the majority, this is undeniable proof that you lack both Genius and Swagger.

❧

Any idiot can see why something shouldn't be done. An achiever with Swagger sees why it should be done and does it!

❧

To the influencer with Raunchy Swagger, fifteen minutes of notoriety beats the best advertising that money can buy.

❧

There is a very thin line between genius and insanity. Characters with Raunchy Swagger make a point of erasing that line.

The less that achievers with Elegant Swagger respond to critics and negative people, the more positive their lives become.

ଔ

When you play for a lot more than you can afford to lose, you know that you have Raunchy Swagger. It does pay off sometimes, however.

ଔ

The character with Swagger who has achieved a measure of success in the past will tell you, "It's better to be a has-been than a never-was."

ଔ

Achievers with Swagger don't march in rank and file unless it will help some important cause for society and the world at large.

Individuals with Elegant Swagger don't inherit their names. They make their names through their own actions that produce remarkable results.

ᘓ

Characters with Raunchy Swagger are not afraid to be outrageous. They know that the pathological critics will try to shoot them down even if they aren't.

ᘓ

There is a big difference between having Swagger and having a bumper sticker on one's car.

ᘓ

Achievers with Swagger will always disregard the advice of individuals experiencing serious difficulties in their lives.

Individuals with Super Swagger have no fear of perfection because they know that no one ever achieves it.

∞

Financial Swagger is having five or more major bank credit cards and never using them for credit but only for convenience and rewards points.

∞

People with Swagger hear the very best advice from the pathological critics and then go away and do the exact opposite.

∞

The individual with Swagger is an adventurous soul. When the ship of the adventurous soul hits the reef of criticism, adversity, and failure — it's the criticism, adversity, and failure that are smashed to bits and pieces — and not the adventurous soul.

Achievers with Swagger don't care whether they win by an inch or a mile. They know that, after all, winning is winning.

ଔ

If characters with Swagger decide to sell fish for a living, they sell big fish — lots of them. That's the secret to their success.

ଔ

After individuals with Swagger have worked hard to get what they want, they take the time to truly enjoy it — with Swagger!

ଔ

Anyone with Swagger who wants to apologize to someone does it in person or by telephone and does not hide behind a text or an email.

Magic happens at the extremes. Achievers with Super Swagger take action of the hell-bent-for-glory type that few people ever take.

☙

If you're not offending a number of people, you are likely not very original and have little or no Swagger.

☙

Haters don't really hate individuals with Swagger. They hate themselves. The individuals with Swagger are a reflection of what they would truly like to be.

☙

Achievers with Swagger are never afraid to tread the path alone. They choose the path on their own and do not follow someone else's footsteps.

A good scare is worth more to the individual with Swagger than general advice from the average person.

❧

If you run into Santa Clause and he asks you for your autograph, you likely have quite a bit of Swagger.

❧

Taking a ton of selfies does not give you Swagger. Never having taken a selfie, on the other hand, gives you Super Swagger.

❧

Individuals with Elegant Swagger dress respectfully when attending church, going to job interviews, and flying Business Class.

Moralists like to talk about the hollowness of success attained by super achievers with Swagger. About the hollowness of their own failures, they are silent.

☙

All sorts of people can have Swagger. Intellectually bright guys can have Swagger and stupid guys can have Swagger. Talented individuals can have Swagger and blockheads can have Swagger. Rich people can have Swagger and poor people can have Swagger. Some degree of ability to think differently and to act boldly is, of course, essential.

☙

The population in general lives vicariously through their favorite movie stars and sports heroes. Achievers with Super Swagger live vicariously through themselves.

Having a major street named after you is Super Swagger. Having a back alley named after you — not so much!

Swagger is more than just a sport. It's a way of life. To be sure, a lifestyle that only a few people ever experience.

❦

Achievers with Swagger who want to become rich do eventually become rich. They are willing to take action to get there. It must be the right type of action, however. The amount of money that they make will always be in direct proportion to the demand for what they do, their ability to do it, and how fast they can do it.

❦

The individual with Swagger who truly loves life feels that life is too short to stuff mushrooms, stand in line, or drive ATVs.

❦

Anything sensational done without Swagger is even more sensational done with Swagger.

Unlike the majority in society, achievers with Swagger actually think. They have 3C Vision based on critical thinking skills, creative thinking skills, and common sense. Therefore, they are somewhat dangerous and a threat to the majority who have 3D Vision, based on delusion, denial, and distortion.

⚘

Just because you consider yourself a badass like Justin Bieber doesn't mean you have Swagger.

⚘

A red-hot idea generated by an achiever with Swagger is one that hits other people with a thundering bolt of envy.

⚘

Insofar as all the important things that the majority of people think but don't say, people with Swagger actually say them.

30

Whenever faced with a major challenge, the achiever with Super Swagger plans carefully and then knocks it out of the park.

⊗

When with friends, the individual with Swagger even makes going to the grocery store an adventure.

⊗

Extraordinary results require time — and time waits for no one. Achievers with Super Swagger know how to use their time on the right projects and put no time into the wrong projects.

⊗

Swagger doesn't come cheap. Remember that a free lunch ain't worth what you paid for it.

If your signature has no Swagger, you likely don't either.

ભ

The smart person with Swagger never listens to financial advice from people who are themselves broke and in debt. It is clear that these full-goose bozos will steer any individuals willing to listen to them off their financial rails.

ભ

Achievers with Swagger attain their success based on service to others and not at the expense of others.

ભ

Individuals with Swagger don't wait around at home hoping to be discovered. They get around town and all over the country to show their great qualities and abilities in action.

If you find yourself as the person with the most Swagger in the room, it's okay to hang out in that room. If you find yourself as the smartest person in that room, however, you should find another room to hang out in.

❧

Raunchy Swagger is a double-edged sword. It will get you in some restaurants a lot quicker but it will also get you thrown out of a few other restaurants a lot quicker.

❧

What's wrong with Swagger? All your comic book heroes had Swagger. Superman had Swagger. Wonderwoman had Swagger. Batman had Swagger. Spider-Man had Swagger. Miss Marvel had Swagger. Why can't you have any Swagger?

The great Boston Bruin NHL player Bobby Orr advised, "Forget about style; worry about results." That's what achievers with Swagger do. They focus on results simply because remarkable results don't lie. Style is irrelevant.

∞

Individuals with Elegant Swagger never allow their dogs to bark and disturb the neighbors. Only certified full-goose bozos do that.

∞

Super Influencers with Swagger generate great content for their business. They know that great content is king — and promotion is the supreme emperor.

Financial Swagger is being able to avoid the cheap seats and instead sitting in the VIP seats at the Proms in the Royal Albert Hall in London or at a Rolling Stones concert at Hyde Park.

Marketing guru Seth Godin said, "It's all about status." For sure, individuals with Swagger have status that individuals without Swagger don't such as sitting in best seats on airplanes. They even sometimes fly Business Class for free.

Individuals with Swagger always play fairly whether they have a winning hand or they don't have a winning hand.

At the horse show, the horse with Swagger gets noticed. All other horses are ignored.

The secret to being an achiever with Swagger, highly successful in business, is to know a lot that hardly anyone else knows.

∝

Elegant Swagger is flying Business Class whenever you fly. Super Swagger is flying Business Class with the seat beside you empty. Raunchy Swagger is refusing to fly and getting off the airplane because your Business Class seat was canceled and a middle seat in economy was assigned to you.

∝

Individuals with Swagger never allow themselves to be so inebriated as to have to slur their words. That would be super-duper-loser embarrassing. Indeed, an embarrassment fit for the certified full-goose bozos of this world.

Elegant Swagger is drinking an Americano at Starbucks. Super Swagger is drinking Death Wish Coffee in Australia. Raunchy Swagger is drinking Cowboy Coffee whether you are on the range, at home, or at Starbucks.

◌ℾ

Individuals with Swagger do not spend time picking fights on Twitter or Facebook. They know that this is a no-results game best left for the certified full-goose bozos of this world to pursue with glee.

◌ℾ

Financial Swagger for super achievers means having multiple streams of income and not only one.

Individuals with Elegant Swagger complain about how others are doing something wrong by quietly going about it by doing that something right. In other words, they complain about bad software by making great software.

৵

Individuals with Elegant Swagger don't feel that a gift is truly theirs until they have acknowledged and thanked the giver.

৵

Having an MBA or PhD does not mean you have Swagger. The person with Swagger, in fact, is one who has an MBA or a PhD and never mentions it to anyone.

৵

When players with Swagger bluff at the poker table, they bluff big time.

Even when characters with Swagger end up doing foolish things, they do these things with enthusiasm.

❧

Individuals with Elegant Swagger keep extra copies of *The Little Prince* by Antoine de Saint-Exupéry to give to kids and adults alike.

❧

Elegant Swagger is driving a Mercedes 2-dr. coupe. Super Swagger is driving an Aston Martin Vanquish 2-dr. coupe. Raunchy Swagger is driving a rusted-out 1995 Camry 2-dr coupe even though your net worth is over $2 million.

❧

When characters with Raunchy Swagger see a snake, they just kill it. They never ask where it came from.

Individuals with Swagger never boast about their family tree. That's best left for people without anything more important to boast about.

ଊ

Achievers with Super Swagger are professionals who expect a lot of criticism. Totally ignoring their critics is their ultimate self-care.

ଊ

Characters with Raunchy Swagger aren't scared to upset the apple cart. The way they look at it, if they don't, the apples in time will rot away anyway.

ଊ

Individuals with Swagger choose style over fashion. Always!

Sometimes to exhibit Elegant Swagger, it is best, as John Wayne said, to "Talk low, talk slow, and don't say much."

∞

The worst waste of breath for the individual with Swagger, aside from trying to play the bagpipes in a rock band, is giving valuable advice to the certified full-goose bozos of this world.

∞

Watching a lot of TV is just a bad habit for which a wise achiever with Swagger allocates no time.

∞

Society is most often a commonwealth of deplorable conformists. That's why individuals with Swagger don't fit in.

Is the product or service you provide to the world remarkable? Is it worth making a positive remark about? If yes, it has Swagger.

∞

The influencer with Swagger who can get a brilliant idea to spread virally will win big time.

∞

The greatest danger for super achievers with Swagger is not that their aim is too high and they will miss it, but that it is too low and they will reach it.

∞

Individuals with Swagger are rarely, if ever, scammed. Legendary gambler Canada Bill Jones once said, "It is morally wrong to allow suckers to keep their money." So, don't be a sucker. Or be one, if you enjoy being fleeced!

Financial Swagger is earning and saving a good portion of your money before you ever consider spending it.

❧

The reason that achievers with financial Swagger still read books about money is the same reason they wound up prosperous in the first place.

❧

People with Swagger will never give any sort of alcoholic drink to a bore. A well-primed bore is one of the hardest things in the world to endure. There is also no off-switch on this creature.

❧

At a wine tasting, the individual with Elegant Swagger will declare either, "The bouquet is better than the taste," or "The taste is better than the bouquet."

Achievers with Swagger don't follow trends; they start trends.

Ê

Characters with Swagger enjoy deceiving the idiots of this world. They speak the truth and the idiots never believe them.

Ê

Financial Swagger is totally owning the house you truly love and having no mortgage on it.

Ê

If you want to exhibit international Swagger, you can't do it just from your hometown — even if your hometown is New York. You will need to visit Paris, London, Prague, Honolulu, Vancouver, Istanbul, and Amsterdam — maybe even Fort McMurray.

Financial Swagger is maintained by keeping an eye on your money like a hawk once you get a lot of it.

☙

The individual with Swagger knows better than to deal with a person who has nothing to lose.

☙

Regardless of the situation, individuals with Elegant Swagger always react with class.

☙

Authors with Swagger who want to be well-known writers such as Ernest Hemingway stop talking about it. They just sit down and get to the business of actually writing sensational books.

To take top billing, achievers with Swagger fight for their most cherished dreams even if, in the words of Paulo Coelho, "that means fighting alone."

☙

Financial Swagger is joyfully paying $50,000 for your friend's hip or knee replacement because he or she can't afford it and it's not covered by their health insurance.

☙

Achievers with Swagger don't walk to the pizza parlor around the corner and consider that a day's exercise. They actually joyfully exercise vigorously for one to two hours a day.

☙

Swagger is vital to the refined character when the rubber hits the road. A Volvo, a Volkswagen, or a Subaru just won't do.

There are many rational arguments for not buying a Porsche *911 Turbo S* — but achievers with Super Swagger don't want to be bored by any of them.

Achievers with Swagger know that many members of society are incapable of hearing the truth, much less of applauding it.

ॐ

The guy with Raunchy Swagger doesn't fret when the certified full-goose bozos of this world criticize him. But he is somewhat concerned when the certified full-goose bozos applaud him.

ॐ

Individuals with Swagger make their birthdays an all-day celebration. They know that studies have shown that birthdays are good for you. Indeed, the more birthdays you have, the longer you will live.

ॐ

A character with Raunchy Swagger will attempt any person's job — but never any horse's job.

Achievers with Swagger never quit. They never explain either. In the end, they just get the job done in extraordinary fashion and let all the pathological critics and hounding habitual haters howl in indignation.

တ

Individuals with Swagger are seldom in concert with general public opinion. That's what makes them so interesting.

တ

The majority regularly indulge in arguments such as how the toilet paper should be hung in the holder. These arguments don't matter — period. Super achievers with Swagger spend their time discussing things that do matter — things they take well-intentioned action on.

Achievers with Swagger know that the key to mastering any thing important requires not only doing the best they can do it, but also doing it the best it can be done.

☗

Individuals with Swagger never exhibit the world-owes-me-a-living syndrome. This is a disease that afflicts the meandering misfits, the crybaby clowns, the babbling bozos, the pathological critics, the perpetual pessimists, the vanquished victims, the no-hoper mopers, and the misinformed muddleheads.

☗

People with Elegant Swagger never underestimate the power of human stupidity. That's why they avoid it as much as possible.

☗

Actors with Swagger always stay in their own special movie.

50

To maximize their opportunities to become prosperous and free, super achievers with Swagger surround themselves with creative and sensational big thinkers.

ଓ

Ambitious individuals with Swagger normally hang around and play with other ambitious individuals who always bring their "A" game to the arena of life.

ଓ

Characters with Swagger are just as careful in lying as they are in telling the truth.

ଓ

Financial Swagger is being able to make a lot of money from your creative works and intellectual property while you sleep.

Individuals with Swagger should not tell too many stories. The problem for an individual with Swagger telling a sensational story is that it always reminds the certified full-goose bozo of an extremely boring one.

◈

Just think how happy you would be if God took away everything you own and after a month gave it back to you. Achievers with Swagger always keep this in mind and constantly experience gratitude for what they have.

◈

Humility may be a noble virtue, but it doesn't help the character with Swagger get waited on in a crowded department store at Christmas.

Achievers with Swagger don't rely on luck to attain success and prosperity. As *Life's Secret Handbook* states, "In the realm of prosperity, luck only favors those adventurous souls who don't expect or rely on luck."

જી

When characters with Raunchy Swagger are told that they are outspoken, they reply, "Oh yeah, by whom?"

જી

The character with Raunchy Swagger doesn't care if what he or she is wearing panics the cat.

જી

Yes, life is short. Nevertheless, achievers with Swagger don't live to avoid death. They live to enjoy life.

Achievers with Swagger lead for a reason. As an old adage advises, "If you ain't the lead dog, the scenery never changes."

☙

Achievers with Swagger always think big. If their original goal is ten, they eventually ask the question, "How can I reach 20?"

☙

Characters with Raunchy Swagger are kind and considerate to others, but depending upon who the others are. They can also be jerks, but only to those who have truly earned it.

☙

Individuals with Super Swagger will sometimes assume a pose, but one that no one has yet discovered.

To the individual with Super Swagger, living life in general must be like making love — it's all or nothing!

ʘ

If achievers with Swagger know something extremely important that all their major competitors don't, they conceal it as well as they can. As Don Shimoda said in Richard Bach's inspirational fable *Illusions*, "Learn what the magician knows and it's not magic anymore."

ʘ

To the individual with Swagger, a little inexactness in a story sometimes saves a ton of explanation.

ʘ

Individuals with Swagger do not dig ditches or make love as their flagship career.

Achievers with Swagger cheer their best friends on when the best friends are totally killing it on their projects, even if they themselves are not doing so well at the moment.

◌

Achievers with Super Swagger hitch their dreams to a speeding star and not to a wavering wagon.

◌

What makes the Swagger individual's vanity so intolerable to other people is that it injures their own. After all, as Elizabeth Smart indicated, "vanity is other people's pride"

◌

Achievers with Financial Swagger feel that it is better to be cheated in price than in quality.

When the polls are in the Swagger guy's favor, he flaunts them. When the polls are not in his favor, he taunts them.

❧

Characters with Swagger normally don't worry about the government in power, and if they do, they don't admit it!

❧

Highly successful achievers with Swagger take the high road while all the bungling creeps, babbling bozos, and pathological critics take the low road.

❧

Individuals with Super Swagger once a year go somewhere in the world to a place they have never been. That's precisely what the Dalai Lama advocated.

Achievers with Super Swagger don't waste time responding to their critics. As Super Swagger guy, the late Frank Sinatra, proclaimed, "I'm convinced they [critics] are descendants of Attila the Hun, Hitler, and Charles Manson."

ଔ

Slothful individuals avoid necessary and even urgent tasks in the workplace by pretending to be busy on important things that are already done. Achievers with Swagger, on the other hand, just get busy on the necessary and urgent tasks and produce results.

ଔ

Doing their best at something trivial is not good enough for achievers with Swagger. They have to be doing their best at important things that can lead to sensational success.

John Otway proclaimed, "There's no point in success if you don't let it go to your head. That's what it's for." To the individual with Swagger, there's also no point in success if you don't tell others about it. Humbly boasting about it to others may just motivate these others to reach much greater heights in life too.

℞

The biggest shortcoming of equality is that most people want it only with those superior to them such as, for example, highly successful individuals with Swagger.

℞

Envy of achievers with Swagger is one of the most foolish human faults given that there is nothing to be gained from it. It is one of the most sincere forms of flattery, however, to the achievers with Swagger.

When the character with Swagger cooks for oneself, he or she ends up complimenting the chef at least three or four times while eating the meal.

❧

Bob Hope in an interview with *Playboy* magazine in 1973 said, "The only time to believe any kind of rating is when it shows you at the top." To be sure, that's the Swagger approach.

❧

You can't emotionally hurt thinking people with Swagger by insulting them because of their great success. They will have already seen this coming. You will just be proving them right in their believing that you are worthy of being totally ignored.

Individuals with Elegant Swagger will never correct a fool because the fool will hate them for it. On the other hand, individuals with Elegant Swagger will correct a wise person because the wise person will appreciate what the individuals with Elegant Swagger have done for him or her.

⚮

Had the woman with Swagger such as Jen Sincero not loved herself, she would never have been inclined to love anything. In other words, self-love to her is the basis of all love.

⚮

To the average person, confidence is merely that quiet, assured feeling one has before one falls flat on one's face. This seldom happens to the achiever with Swagger.

Even when achievers with Swagger wind up in the gutter, they still confidently gaze at the stars.

☙

Extraordinary prosperous individuals with Super Swagger are known to have trained themselves for lucrative professions that didn't even exist.

☙

For the achiever with Elegant Swagger, as Paulo Coelho pointed out, "Life is the train, not the station."

☙

Characters with Raunchy Swagger are well seasoned. If they are thrown out of Heaven, they will show their Swagger in whatever other place they end up at.

Individuals with Swagger a long time ago realized that waiting at home for opportunity to knock is like standing at the bus depot waiting for their ship to come into port.

ଜ

Moralists and losers who despise successful individuals with Swagger are joyfully tolerant of any person who has absolutely no talent and is excessively modest about it.

ଜ

An achiever with Swagger never complains about the lack of opportunity in this world. That's best left for the certified full-goose bozos that have infiltrated the Internet.

ଜ

The ability to change a car tire adds to a person's Swagger.

Impeccable punctuality is a sign of Swagger. The lack of it is a sure sign of the lack of Swagger as well as the lack of respect for others.

❧

Swagger has nothing to do with putting cute messages on answering machines or cell phones.

❧

The character with Swagger feels that Mark Twain was right when he said, "There are no grades of vanity; there are only grades of ability in concealing it."

❧

Financial Swagger is having big bucks in the bank. Just ask super achievers Warren Buffet and Kevin O'Leary.

A financial advisor with Swagger such as Kevin O'Leary will happily recommend the international bestseller *How to Retire Happy, Wild and Free: Retirement Wisdom That You Won't Get from Your Financial Advisor* to his clients and friends.

Achievers with Swagger don't follow the crowd. They know that if they follow the crowd, they will get no further than the crowd. That's not a good place to be.

രു

Individuals with financial Swagger always pay their bills on time — no exceptions!

രു

Whatever is truly impossible for achievers with Swagger to accomplish never interferes with what they can accomplish.

രു

Just because something seems impossible for everyone else doesn't mean that the achiever with Swagger can't accomplish it.

Fathers and mothers with Swagger never skimp on their lifestyle to leave money in their will for their adult children.

∞

Super Swagger is being tough minded — but tender hearted — to one's children.

∞

The character with Swagger may have some inner madness but keeps it under lock and key.

∞

To the individual with Raunchy Swagger, nothing matters very much, and few things matter at all.

∞

Having Swagger means not being deceived by first impressions.

Elegant Swagger: To be infected with a high degree of intellectual independence; not conforming to society's standards of behavior, speech, and actions, at odds with the vast majority, but at the same time still making a big positive difference in this world that the vast majority is not making.

☙

An individual with Raunchy Swagger could have said, "It is a very noble hypocrisy not to talk of oneself." It wasn't — it was German philosopher Friedrich Wilhelm Nietzsche who said this.

☙

Having Elegant Swagger means that you never cheat at anything — ever!

☙

People with Swagger never mention being in debt or on a diet.

Achievers with Swagger always over tip restaurant servers when the service is remarkable.

Individuals with Swagger never humbly boast to anyone that they are vegans — even if they are.

If the woman with Super Swagger makes herself a spinach salad, she does it with colorful flair. She adds strawberries, blueberries, black grapes, carrots, red peppers, and green apples.

Intelligent people with Swagger know how far to go with their intelligence without going too far. When you let certain people know how much more common sense you have than they do, they will not want to have anything to do with you.

Achievers with financial Swagger know how to read a company financial report and know the difference between debt and deficit. Most people in the US and Canada don't.

Super achievers with Swagger never blame others, society, or the government. They take 100 percent responsibility for every area of their lives and get results that others don't.

Individuals with true Swagger don't mess with drugs and will have nothing to do with those who do.

Super Swagger in business means promising big and delivering even bigger.

The character with Swagger may end up on the wrong train but does not whine and instead makes the best of it.

Swagger means having a firm — but not brutal — handshake.

Guys with Swagger don't stoop to shooting defenseless animals and birds in an attempt to prove their manhood.

At fine restaurants, individuals with Super Swagger normally pay cash. If they don't, they use a high-end American Express card.

Music lovers with Elegant Swagger own a great stereo system.

Regardless of how dire the situation, people with Swagger keep their cool.

ଔ

Achievers with Swagger follow *The Four Agreements* as advocated by Don Miguel Ruiz in his book with that name. 1. Don't make assumptions. 2. Don't take things personally. 3. Be impeccable with your word. 4. Always do your best.

ଔ

Financial Swagger is having enough money for all your needs and a lot of your wants.

ଔ

Living with a high achiever with Swagger is easier but less satisfying than being one.

Individuals with Super Swagger buy a lot of great books — even if they never read all of them.

Successful achievers with Swagger demand excellence in anything they purchase and are willing to pay for it. They are proof of the adage: Those who pay the most complain the least.

Using the "F" word constantly does not give you Swagger. It does just the opposite. It makes you sound swaggerless.

Achievers with Swagger don't work in an office without windows. They know that they deserve better.

Expensive champagne is often enjoyed by super achievers with Swagger for no reason at all.

Cℛ

Committees are not a place for achievers with Swagger. New, sensational, world-changing ideas normally come from one creative person working alone.

Cℛ

Singing joyfully in the shower every day shows that you have at least a bit of Swagger.

Cℛ

When approached by news reporters, individuals with Swagger who don't want to be mentioned in their local newspaper say, "No comment. But that's off the record, so don't quote me on this."

74

Individuals with Super Swagger are the first to say hello.

છ

Unacceptable behavior is never accepted by anyone with Swagger. They either confront it or walk away.

છ

Individuals with Swagger take out the garbage without being told and when no one sees them doing it.

છ

Swagger in general means showing ultimate respect for police officers, fire fighters, and military personnel.

છ

Integrity is never exchanged for money, power, or fame by individuals with genuine Swagger.

If individuals with Swagger take an over night train trip, they don't cheap out. They sleep in a Pullman-type parlor car.

☙

Achievers with Swagger hang up on anyone who puts them on hold to take another call.

☙

Learning the "tricks of the trade" is for losers. Learning the trade in excellence is for achievers with Swagger. Fact is, you can't "fake it until you make it." And if you fake it and make it, you are still a fake. A genuine fraud, in other words.

☙

Financial Swagger to the super achiever is being able to retire in prosperity without needing any form of government assistance.

Individuals with Super Swagger use the good silver even when dining alone at home.

Achievers with Elegant Swagger can identify the music of Chopin, Mozart, or Beethoven if it is being played in a fine restaurant.

Individuals with Swagger are never ashamed of their own true patriotism but they also know that an appeal to patriotism is the last refuge of loud mouth politicians who have nothing better or more constructive to say.

Swagger is best shown by being a self-starter at anything you do and never giving excuses for why you didn't make the attempt.

Achievers with Swagger always pay their fair share — often even a lot more than their fair share — when dining with others.

ରଙ

Winners with Swagger do what losers don't want to do. They know that if they don't, trouble will increase at an exponential rate like it does for the losers of this world.

ରଙ

In business, Swagger means cheerfully giving your clients your enthusiastic best.

ରଙ

Characters with Raunchy Swagger occasionally play Monopoly — but only with real money. They also occasionally enter tractor pulling contests — but only against the tractor.

Financial Swagger is splurging on things that you don't need, confident you have enough money to pay for everything without having to go in debt for anything.

❧

Pushing your luck at times shows that you have at least a bit of Swagger.

❧

When characters with Raunchy Swagger have to choose between two sensational experiences, they will always choose the one they haven't tried.

❧

Achievers with Swagger know that they must be strong enough to admit their mistakes, intelligent enough to profit from them, and industrious enough to correct them.

Individuals with Swagger live their lives as an exclamation and not as an explanation.

∞

Financial Swagger is having a nice nest egg and no debt.

∞

Super Swagger entails the willingness to happily and confidently lose minor battles in order to win the major wars.

∞

Intelligent individuals with Swagger never pay for work before it is completed.

∞

Individuals with Elegant Swagger don't feel that a gift is truly theirs until they have acknowledged and thanked the giver.

Highly accomplished individuals with Swagger judge their own success by what they had to give up in order to attain it.

Achievers with Super Swagger know how to grind it out when others won't. Hanging on just a little longer than the competition often makes them winners.

Always impeccably keeping promises is an essential standard for having Super Swagger and being a success in business.

Again, achievers with Swagger never apologize to anyone for their own remarkable success. Why would they? That would be as ridiculous as apologizing for being alive.

Achievers with Swagger are grateful for their position in life and feel there is always something to be thankful for.

&

Prosperous individuals with Swagger may have a few prize possessions but they never let these possessions possess them.

&

Individuals with Elegant Swagger are never afraid to say "I'm sorry", "I made a mistake", "I don't know", or "I would like more time to think it over."

&

Taking the stairs when it's four flights or less is an important Swagger move that will impress others and bless you with some great health benefits.

Individuals with Elegant Swagger never give a gift that's not handsomely wrapped.

વ્ર

Prosperous individuals with financial Swagger save at least 10 percent of their income. In fact, that's for amateurs. The pros save a lot more — normally 25 percent or higher.

વ્ર

Beige cars have absolutely nothing to do with Swagger.

વ્ર

When achievers with Swagger lose big time, they don't lose the big lesson.

વ્ર

Super achievers with Swagger are never laid back.

Individuals with Elegant Swagger always arrive early for a business appointment and never apologize for it.

❧

Dressing better than your clients is an important Swagger move.

❧

Business people with Swagger read the *New York Times*, *Washington Post*, *Financial Times*, and *Wall Street Journal*.

❧

Swagger means always doing the right thing regardless of what the majority thinks or does.

❧

If you don't have at least a bit of Swagger — your life story will not make a good book. Don't even try!

Of all the ethnic foods in the world, Italian food has the most Swagger. The problem with Italian food, however, is that you are hungry again in two or three days.

Individuals with any degree of Financial Swagger don't dine at buffet type restaurants.

☙

Big problems are welcomed by individuals with Swagger because these problems carry with them big opportunities.

☙

Thinking quickly and talking slowly is the Elegant Swagger way to converse with others.

☙

Doing it right the first time and not saying anything is much more of a Swagger move than messing it up the first time and offering a lot of excuses why you messed up.

Becoming someone's true hero is one of the goals of the individual with Elegant Swagger.

☙

When asked to play the piano or the saxophone, the musician with Swagger does it without complaining or making excuses.

☙

When business people with Swagger go to borrow money from the bank, they dress like they have plenty of it.

☙

Individuals with Elegant Swagger never take the last cookie or the last piece of fried chicken at a family gathering.

Super achievers with Swagger don't conceptualize; they think.

❧

Unlike a significant segment of society, achievers with Swagger never did join the Book-of-the-Month Club. They were smart enough to choose great books on their own.

❧

Word has it that Justin Bieber hired a Swagger coach for three years. If he wanted more Swagger, he shouldn't have gotten sixty tattoos. Contrary to popular belief, the fewer tattoos you get, the more Swagger you will have.

❧

The guy with Raunchy Swagger always buys the big bottle of Tabasco.

Some rich guys like to dine with Swagger. Nuar Gulbenkian, British oil tycoon and socialite, no doubt had Swagger when it came to dining. He professed, "The best number for a dinner party is two — myself and a dam' good head waiter."

⚭

Sometimes achievers with Super Swagger encounter major difficulties, not because they're doing something drastically wrong, but because they're doing something spectacularly right.

⚭

Owning gold gives you Financial Swagger, much more so than having a lot of debt. In this regard Norm Franz advised, "Gold is the money of kings; silver is the money of gentlemen; barter is the money of peasants; but debt is the money of slaves."

The leader with Swagger is someone who is going somewhere important and is able to convince other people to get on board.

ରଛ

Having Swagger, above all, means relying on your own thinking. Individuals with Swagger depend wholly on themselves by doing things in accordance with their own way of thinking and principles and not based on the thinking and principles of other people or society. To be dependent on the opinions and tastes of others is to be a slave to society.

ରଛ

Achievers with Swagger will invent something that no one else has invented. If it is immediately criticized by the vast majority — this proves the Genius of their design.

Achievers with Swagger deliver work that's remarkable. In other words, it's work worth making remarks about! This spreads the word.

☘

Courage is one of the most important virtues of the individual with Swagger. "Without courage," advised Winston Churchill, "all other virtues lose their meaning."

☘

We must meet practically all of life's greatest tests alone. That's why the achiever with Swagger lives by the motto, "If it is to be, it is entirely up to me."

☘

Individuals with Swagger don't lay raps on others.

People with Swagger enjoy spending a lot of time alone. As spiritual writer Dr. Wayne Dyer once said, "You cannot be lonely if you like the person that you are alone with."

℞

The individual with Elegant Swagger is just as friendly and respectful to the janitor as to the President of the company.

℞

Achievers with Swagger are quick to take advantage of an opportunity that most people won't ever see.

℞

When individuals with Swagger require professional advice, they get it from highly-paid professionals and not from their friends or acquaintances.

The single individual shows Swagger by purchasing an expensive king-size bed with an expensive organic mattress and then happily sleeps diagonally on it every night.

ର

Silence is often the best answer by the individual with Swagger when asked a question by an idiot.

ର

Achievers with Swagger perform their jobs better than anyone else can. They realize that it's the best job security they can create for themselves.

ର

Individuals with Swagger don't believe in being right at all costs. Only losers do this. It's the proverbial case of winning the battle but losing the war.

Super achievers with Swagger learn more from a fool than the fool learns from them.

ର

The more achievers with Swagger know about this world, the less they fear about it.

ର

There is no amount of money available that can coerce an achiever with Swagger to work at a job that he or she despises.

ର

Libertarians with Swagger know that the supply of government far exceeds demand. That's one of the reasons they stay away from working in government.

Individuals with Swagger never lie down with a member of the opposite sex who has more problems than they do.

❧

Super achievers with Swagger never say anything like, "I'm trying to get my act together" or "I'm finally mellowing out."

❧

Individuals with Elegant Swagger are wise with their money and expect their friends and spouses to be the same. They know that people who are foolish with their money are foolish in many other ways too.

❧

Baseball players with Swagger such as Reggie Jackson would rather strike out than take a base-on-balls.

High achievers with Swagger never cut corners even if they believe no one will notice.

❧

The individual with Swagger does not live on hope alone. As the famous American scientist and writer Benjamin Franklin observed, "He that lives upon hope will die fasting."

❧

Even if others consider him or her an eccentric, the person with Swagger is always original and does not ever try to imitate someone else.

❧

Individuals with Super Swagger never let weeds grow around their sensational dreams.

Achievers with Super Swagger hold themselves to the highest standards — and often exceed them.

☙

A person with real Swagger would never stop a major parade to pick up a dollar or even 100 dollars. That's best left for the those in this world suffering from poverty consciousness. It can be said that these people are being trite in a very obnoxious way.

☙

When the character with Raunchy Swagger comes up with a brilliant idea while with others, he or she sometimes quips, "See, there is no off-switch on this Genius machine!"

☙

Individuals with Financial Swagger don't buy life insurance or flight insurance.

Again, women can have Swagger too. With her exceptional talent and Swagger, super achiever Tina Turner proved to the world that music produces a sensational enjoyment that most humans cannot do without.

Achievers in business with Super Swagger have their own WOW factor! This applies to both the service that they provide to the world and the way they market it. They make it edgy, they make it snappy, and they make it punchy. They may even make it Raunchy — but they make it Different! Real Different!

Making the simple complex doesn't exhibit Swagger. Making the complex simple, now, that's Swagger!

To the general population a narcissist is any super high achiever with Swagger who is much more prosperous and successful than they are.

Super achievers with Swagger don't major in minor things.

Individuals with Swagger tend to be great spirits not necessarily in tune with the majority in society. "Great spirits," observed Albert Einstein, "have always encountered violent opposition from mediocre minds."

∞

"People who are crazy enough to think they can change the world," stated Apple's 1997 ad campaign, "are the only ones who do." Think Einstein. Think Picasso. Think Gandhi. Think Arden. Think Jobs. Think Musk. Indeed, all of these crazy, remarkable individuals had their own brand of Swagger.

∞

"A lack of Swagger can be a problem," observed author and blogger Charlie Hoehn, "because it prevents you from living your fullest potential."

People with Swagger give generously to charities, much more than the vast majority does, without thought of the return. In this regard, Duc François de La Rochefoucauld, stated, "Plenty of people despise money, but few know how to give it away."

◌ℜ

The creative self-employed achiever with Super Swagger is capable of more accomplishment and success alone than a team of 100 corporate sociopaths are capable of together

◌ℜ

Life is a game. Happy people are the players. Unhappy people are the spectators. In this regard, individuals with Swagger are always the most eager players.

101

When people with Swagger do something wrong to someone and realize that they have, they apologize immediately without anyone first demanding an apology. As Judge Robert Drain ruled in the Sackler family/Purdue Pharma court case, "A forced apology is not really an apology."

☙

When individuals with Swagger find something they really want, they don't let a few dollars keep them from buying it.

☙

Achievers with Swagger go to bed when they want to go to bed and get up when they want to get up. They know that studies have concluded that successful people wake up whenever they decide to and night owls tend to perform better on measures of memory, processing speed, and cognitive ability.

The single individual with Swagger knows that being with no one is much better than being with the wrong ones. Often those who fly solo have the strongest wings.

∞

On particularly tough days, super achievers with Swagger remind themselves that their track record for getting through bad days is 100 percent — and that's damn good!

∞

In order to attain the impossible, the character with Raunchy Swagger attempts the absurd.

∞

All individuals with Swagger know that other people's negativity isn't worth worrying about.

Millions of people don't like exercising vigorously because it cramps their lifestyle. Super achievers with Swagger like exercising vigorously because it enhances their lifestyle.

ᑿ

Achievers with Swagger always charge for their professional work, even for friends and relatives. They know that most people don't value what they don't pay for.

ᑿ

Immeasurable power is to be found in being a non-conformist. Individuals with Swagger realize, as J. Paul Getty said, "No one can possibly achieve any real and lasting success or 'get rich' in business by being a conformist."

Creative spirit is the foundation of all Elegant Swagger. When money is lost, a little is lost. When time is lost, much more is lost. When health is lost, practically everything is lost. And when creative spirit is lost, there is nothing left.

☙

Individuals with Swagger sometimes have to burn a few bridges to prevent the crazies from following them.

☙

Jazz music is for characters with Elegant Swagger. Rock and Roll music is for characters with Super Swagger. Blues music is for characters with Raunchy Swagger. Characters who have an exquisite taste of music enjoy all three equally.

Extreme measures are taken by individuals with Swagger when defending their principles, their standards, and their integrity. They never apologize for this either.

Even when flying Business Class or First Class, you display absolutely no Swagger when you enter the cabin and talk so loudly on your cell phone that everyone in the cabin hears your conversation. In fact, this is the opposite of Swagger. If your excuse is that you have a loud voice, fill your mouth with wet toilet paper. This will do the trick. The flight attendants will be more than happy to provide the wet toilet paper to you for free.

Letting some things remain mysterious is not a weakness for those with Elegant Swagger. It enhances their lives.

Super achievers with Swagger never go looking for trouble. As the wise mountain man advised, "Don't mess with what's not bothering you."

୧

Famous achievers with Swagger have become famous by completing important, difficult tasks that the majority are not willing to undertake.

୧

Some nights the guy with Raunchy Swagger may not feel like going out but his hair looks too good to stay home. So he goes out.

୧

People with Swagger never ignore evil. They confront it.

107

Happiness for the individual with Swagger can be enhanced by others, but does not depend on others.

People with Swagger never try to live out their athletic fantasies through their children. That's best left for the blokes without any major accomplishments and success in their own lives.

Arrested development in the guy with Raunchy Swagger is not as serious as it seems to others. He gets to keep his youth much longer.

An artist with Swagger in the process of painting a picture knows when to stop. Less is often more — sometimes a lot more!

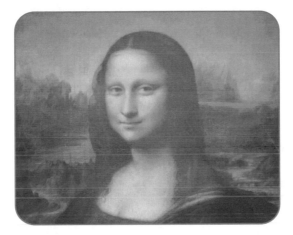

The moment you declare that a particular work of art such Leonardo da Vinci's Mona Lisa has Elegant Swagger, the blowhard elitist artist will tell you that you have no idea what you are talking about.

Those with Super Swagger always purchase a coffee table that they can put their feet on.

⍟

Age is no barrier to Swagger. Some kids have Swagger, some teens have Swagger, and some adults have Swagger. Best of all, some older people have Super Swagger.

⍟

Achievers with Swagger follow their own star and not someone else's.

⍟

You can climb Mount Everest once to prove you have Swagger. Attempt to climb it twice and you will be thought a fool.

110

The super achiever with Swagger just chuckles when people claim they have no ego and tells them, "Ego helps people put bread on the table. Ego also helps people like me create a highly prosperous lifestyle and pay a lot of income tax so people like you can live better than you would otherwise live."

◌঵

There is not one shred of evidence to support the notion that ultimate security is attainable. Thus, individuals with Swagger seek sensational adventure and not ultimate security.

◌঵

Sometimes individuals with Elegant Swagger turn certain enemies into friends by doing something sensational for them.

The individual with Swagger is never shamed by others who call him selfish. He knows that certain people will call him selfish, not for pursuing his own good, but for neglecting something that they want from him. Obviously, their motivation is none other than their own extreme selfishness. Oscar Wilde articulated this point ever so eloquently with his classic statement: "Selfishness is not living as one wishes to live; it is asking others to live as one wishes to live."

∞

The creative chef with Swagger knows that creativity varies inversely with the number of cooks involved with the broth. So she works alone to create her award-winning cuisine.

Individuals with Super Swagger don't play video games, darts, backgammon, pickleball, cricket, Frisbee, or miniature golf.

∞

Individuals with Super Swagger skydive, ski jump, mountain climb, dive off cliffs, hang-glide, shoot the rapids, and sail around the world solo.

∞

Be absolutely clear that you can't outtalk the individual with Swagger who knows what he or she is talking about.

∞

Achievers with Swagger are not afraid of making mistakes. After all, Columbus found America by mistake.

The lazy industrious individual with Swagger will always find an easier and faster way to do something difficult.

෴

If you can keep your head up while all around you are losing theirs, it could be because of your Swagger. On the other hand, you may have misunderstood the situation.

෴

Achievers with Swagger take the time to climb that high mountain they have always wanted to because they know that in the end they won't remember the time they spent working overtime in the office or mowing the lawn when it didn't need mowing.

Swagger is not — as mundane people would want us to believe — a form of insanity. It is often a kind of valuable inner pride of the individual of genius, who is frequently regarded as an undesirable because the individual of genius is entirely unafraid of and uninfluenced by the opinions and mediocrity of the crowd.

ભ

The highly successful person with Swagger makes it a habit of doing what failing people don't like doing.

ભ

The Holy Grail of Financial Swagger is being able to take care of yourself totally from the proceeds of your creative efforts and not being a financial burden on others.

Achievers with Swagger raise their standard of living by raising their standard of thinking, their standard of performance, and their standard of results.

◈

The individual with Super Swagger is the one who normally starts the standing ovation at the end of a play or concert.

◈

Achievers with Swagger are the first there when friends or relatives need them, without having been asked to do so.

◈

The successful little person is treated by the individual with Swagger with the same measure of respect as the successful big person is treated.

"Nowhere can I think so happily as in a train," professed British children books writer A. Milne. That's one of the main reasons authors with Swagger take exotic train rides such as the Rocky Mountaineer in the Canadian Rockies and the Blue Train in South Africa.

◌

Achievers with Swagger stand out from the crowd for a reason. They exude a special self-confidence — directness and courage in meeting reality and the facts of life.

◌

Individuals with Swagger don't have any interest in bickering over small things. Fact is, small things are the focus of small minds.

Without self-confidence, one has no Swagger. "What's the point of self-confidence?" one may ask. Simply put, a healthy degree of self-confidence is the key to leading a productive and rewarding life.

☯

Cartoon characters with Swagger know how to embellish a bad situation and make it sound promising. Calvin in Bill Waterson's famous cartoon *Calvin and Hobbes*, for example, remarked, "You know how Einstein got bad grades as a kid? Well, mine are even worse."

☯

To individuals with Swagger, it doesn't matter what makes sense to the average person. What matters is what brings results that lead to a happy, prosperous, and free life.

Elizabeth Arden's beauty salon grew into an international cosmetics giant. She once remarked, "There's only one Elizabeth like me and that's the Queen." Now, that's a super achiever who knows how to make a Swagger statement!

∞

In another Swagger move, Elizabeth Arden warned her annoying husband, "Dear, never forget one little point. It's my business. You just work here." Only super achievers with remarkable Swagger can talk this way to their spouse.

∞

Achievers with Swagger give generously to charities. Indeed, they give a lot more than the average given by the rest of society and are not afraid to let others know that they do. Hopefully, others may be inspired to do the same.

The bookshelf owned by a super achiever with Swagger is likely to hold *Illusions* by Richard Bach, *How Successful People Think* by John C. Maxwell, *Million Dollar Habits* by Robert J. Ringer, *The Power of Now* by Ekhart Tolle, *The Little Prince* by Antoine de Saint-Exupéry, *The Four Agreements* by Don Miguel Ruiz, and *You Are a Badass* by Jen Sincero.

When the author with Super Swagger writes a book, it's remarkable. In other words, it's worth for the reader to make sensational remarks about. The ensuing word-of-mouth advertising ends up making it a true bestseller.

☙

With print-on-demand self-publishing, anyone can afford to preach in the desert today. True, a book gives an achiever more credibility. But authors with Super Swagger are ones who sell at least 1,000,000 copies of their self-published titles.

☙

Claiming you are an "Amazon Bestselling Author" does not give you Swagger. It makes you look like a genuine fraud because the vast majority of authors making this claim have sold fewer than 500 — or even 100 — copies of their books.

Super achievers with Swagger consider it their duty to tell the truth and in doing so keep in mind these words of Mohandas Gandhi: "Many people, especially ignorant people, want to punish you for speaking the truth, for being correct, for being you. Never apologize for being correct, or for being years ahead of your time. If you're right and you know it, speak your mind. Speak your mind even if you are a minority of one. The truth is still the truth."

〇〉

Achievers with Super Swagger never retreat; they just advance in another direction.

〇〉

Swagger is infuriating to the masses only when done right.

A genuine sense of humor is the pole that adds balance to the steps of the individual with Swagger as she walks the tightrope of life.

ର

Individuals with Swagger take time to cultivate special friendships and once developed, they sustain them as if their lives depend on it — because their lives do depend on it.

ର

Super achievers know how to answer imposing questions with Swagger. When the Canadian Prime Minister Pierre Elliott Trudeau was told by a reporter that US President Richard Nixon had called him an asshole, Trudeau replied, "Look, I have been called a lot worse names by much better people than him."

Individuals with Swagger can be very happy but at the same time they try to make a big positive difference in this world. Happiness in itself is not the goal. As Charles Gow so accurately indicated, "Many people are extremely happy, but are absolutely worthless to society."

೧

The achiever with Swagger serves hors d'oeuvres and fine wine to special guests and not potato chips and beer.

೧

Swagger is about humor, creativity, intelligence, and mystique. If you have it, you will stand out from the rest of the crowd like the person with critical thinking skills at a Donald Trump rally. If your head sticks up above the crowd, however, expect a lot more criticism than praise.

Let's face it. If you want to get into show business big time, Swagger matters. An actor must have Swagger — lots of it! Otherwise, he's nothing. This applies even if all he desires is to co-star in a western comedy like James Coburn did alongside Kirk Douglas in *Draw*.

ଔ

While others add up their troubles, achievers with Swagger count their blessings. They also offer thanks for all the troubles they don't have.

ଔ

People with true Swagger are secure enough to have brand labels inside their clothing and never on the outside. They avoid looking like a walking billboard for Nike, Hugo Boss, Chanel, Ralph Lauren, Prada, or any other brand.

Ordinary people confess their little faults to con others into believing they have no big ones. Successful individuals with Swagger confess their big faults knowing that their own remarkable accomplishments are enough for other super achievers to forget about all their faults.

ॐ

The super achiever with Swagger knows that knowledge in itself is not worth very much without action. As the Buddhists say, "To know and not to do — is still not to know!"

ॐ

Life's a breeze to individuals with Swagger because they work as hard at simplifying it as the vast majority works at complicating it.

A super achieving author with Swagger will self-plagiarize by stealing material from his previous book to make his new book even more remarkable.

◌◌

Financial Swagger is being able to regularly treat your not-so-well-off friends to dinner and fine wine at swanky restaurants.

◌◌

Super achievers with Swagger realize that people are only as rich as the enrichment they bring to the world around them.

◌◌

Achievers with Swagger know that if they want to keep their best friends, they should never go into business with them.

127

According to an Italian proverb, "The best way to get praise is to die." This may be true for most people but not so for men and women with Swagger. The best way to get praise for them is to make a big positive difference in this world while they are alive.

༒

To the achiever with Swagger, there is more happiness and satisfaction from being a first-rate bus driver than a fifth-rate university professor.

༒

Choice powered by superb critical thinking and well-intentioned action — not chance or luck — determines the destiny of the super achiever with Swagger.

The super achiever with Swagger will never lend money to a friend who is not good with money. That's a sure-fire way of losing both.

ભ્ર

Semi-blessed may be those who have no Swagger and cannot be forced to show it.

ભ્ર

Achievers with Swagger often laugh at their problems. They know that if they can laugh at their problems, they can surely live with their problems.

ભ્ર

Super achievers with Swagger never change themselves for anyone. This would be selling themselves short.

No matter how bleak or dark things get, super achievers with Swagger never give up unless the things they give up on are not that important to the higher order of the Universe.

℘

Swagger is to excitedly express your true self in life and in all the things that you do. What's wrong with that?

℘

If an individual with Swagger is accused of having a big ego, the response is, "Yes I have a big ego. But I have never taken a selfie in my whole life and no doubt you have taken many. So who has the bigger ego?"

Achievers with Elegant Swagger will attempt once a year to take a multi-millionaire out to lunch to learn more about success and handling money. They will not cheap out on the cost of the dinner. Cheaping out is definitely a not a Swagger move.

ᘉ

In the remarkable works of genius by an individual with Swagger, others recognize ideas once rejected by themselves.

ᘉ

The super achiever with Swagger may not have the mother of all showers every day — but nevertheless has a damn good shower every day.

A big part of the Swagger individual's total knowledge consists of being ignorant of things that are not worth knowing. Winning a trivia contest is surely not on the list of things to accomplish.

☙

Money which you have not had the trouble of earning from your own creative efforts does not give you Swagger. It makes you a net taker and not a net producer in society. We need a lot more producers and far fewer takers if our governments are to get out of big time debt and continue to provide services to those truly in need.

☙

Individuals with Swagger let others know what they stand for. Equally important, they also let others know what they won't stand for.

Complaining about an airplane flight being delayed for mechanical or other reasons is not a Swagger statement. The airline personnel are doing their very best under the respective circumstances to get you to your destination and as fast as possible. Complimenting the airline personnel for being so careful is a Swagger move.

છ

Achievers with Swagger read only their own mail and never open anyone else's mail.

છ

Super achievers with Swagger spend at least ten times as much time praising their successful friends and acquaintances as they do criticizing them, if they criticize them at all.

Creative individuals with Swagger are not afraid of any controversy generated by their ideas. As observed by American investigative journalist George Seldes, "All great ideas are controversial, or have been at one time."

∞

Individuals with Elegant Swagger never complain about the music in someone else's car when they have been given the opportunity to ride in it. They also never allow anyone to shame or intimidate them about the music selection in their own car.

∞

Achievers with Swagger are smart when they start their own business. They start the businesses on a shoe string budget and keep their expenses in tow. As marketing guru Seth Godin advised, "It pays to have big dreams but low overhead."

Musicians with Swagger are quick to compliment other musicians with Swagger. For example, Axl Rose of Guns and Roses stated, "Mick Jagger is one of the greatest athletes who ever lived, just for how much he puts into it onstage."

Individuals with Swagger know that there is more to life than listening to the spectacular Rolling Stones. There's also listening to the remarkable Beatles, the extraordinary Eagles, the wonderful Who, the outstanding Doors, and the exceptional Bruce Springsteen.

☙

Financial Swagger is being able to work at what you enjoy without having to rely on an income from it.

☙

The negative, critical person who says it cannot be done should never interfere with the super achiever with Swagger who is already in the process of completing it.

"Diverger" is a good word to describe the super achiever with Swagger. "Divergers are less interested in success, more interested in self-expression," claimed prominent American psychologist Leona Tyler. "They chose unusual occupations, such as inventor or entertainer, rather than the more conventional doctor or lawyer."

☙

To the character with Raunchy Swagger, getting kicked out of the Democrat or Republican political party is like getting kicked out of the Book-of-the-Month Club.

☙

Individuals with Elegant Swagger are never too busy to help a handicapped person cross the street.

Super Swagger for an achiever is always finishing projects a long time before they are due.

ରେ

Individuals with Swagger expect to be criticized. Everyone gets criticized. No one is perfect. Of course, the pathological critics are the least perfect of them all.

ରେ

Achievers with Swagger accept failure and success with equal grace. They know that failure isn't anywhere as tragic as the mind makes it out to be.

ରେ

Individuals with Swagger are generous with their expressions of gratitude and appreciation.

When authors with Super Swagger have a book launch, they do it for two or three new books — not only one!

◌ଈ

The individual with Super Swagger lives like the Toltec civilization lived. He has his own truth and lives his own truth. He becomes wise, he becomes wild, and he becomes free.

◌ଈ

Achievers with Swagger never miss an opportunity to meet a President or Prime Minister of their respective country even if they didn't vote for him or her. That's true patriotism!

◌ଈ

Visits by relatives always give pleasure to characters with Raunchy Swagger, if not in the arrival, then on the departure.

139

Artists with Swagger listen carefully to the first criticisms of their work. They particularly pay attention to parts of their work the critics dislike and then decide that those parts are worth keeping and even enhancing.

⚖

The super achiever with Swagger who does not work hard for a living has a creative scheme that does work.

⚖

Financial Swagger is having great residual income from intellectual property that keeps flowing for years.

⚖

If individuals with Super Swagger work for an organization, they work for one where the expectations of them are high and they can do work worthy of recognition.

Achievers with Swagger are known to work diligently. But they also know how to enjoy leisure diligently. In the words of Benjamin Disraeli, "Increased means and increased leisure are the civilizers of man."

ಣ

A great work-life balance is a sign of Swagger. Taking all of one's vacation time and wholeheartedly enjoying every minute of it is the only way to live prosperous and free.

ಣ

To show his gratitude, a married achiever with Swagger sends his mother-in-law flowers on his wife's birthday.

ಣ

If individuals with Swagger are asked to estimate a person's salary, they always intentionally overestimate.

"Whatever you may be sure of," advised James Russell Lowell, "be sure of this — that you are dreadfully like other people." Unless, of course, you have Swagger.

All individuals with Swagger revere and admire creativity. The products and results of creative individuals set them apart from the products and results of other human beings.

High achievers with Swagger are pleased when they discover truth; fools when they discover falsehood.

When the adventurous character with Super Swagger has a four-course meal, it's a different course at four different restaurants.

People with Super Swagger don't cheap out when buying dinner for great friends. Neither do people with Elegant Swagger or Raunchy Swagger.

ରୡ

When in the company of fools, the intelligent individual with Swagger listens most to those who say the least.

ରୡ

When achievers with Swagger find a job they like, they give it everything they've got — sometimes more!

ରୡ

Mel Brooks in his screenplay for The Producers, said, "That's it baby! When you got it, flaunt it! Flaunt it!" Yeah, why not? That's called Swagger.

The successful writer with Swagger is not afraid of offending readers. As renowned author John Locke advised, "If you're not offending a significant number of readers, your writing is probably not very original."

൦ൠ

Super achievers with Swagger would never expect winning results from the losing behavior that the certified full-goose bozos of this world persist in.

൦ൠ

The super achiever with Swagger successful in business lives by this important motto: Be first, be daring, and be different.

൦ൠ

When the going gets tough, everyone disappears except for the super achiever with Swagger.

People with Swagger are good to others but they don't expect much gratitude in return. They know that good deeds are seldom remembered and bad deeds are seldom forgotten.

Authors with Super Swagger use their remarkable talent for writing and their incredible genius for living life to the fullest.

Individuals with Super Swagger stand above the crowd — even if they have to stand alone. There is no greater way to gain self-respect and the respect of the successful and accomplished people in this world.

Healthy men and women with Swagger eat moderately and exercise vigorously.

When economists announce that the year ahead will reward only the truly innovative and industrious workers, this is a frightening outlook for most workers in society. On the other hand, super achievers with Swagger are stoked.

☞

The individual with Swagger never enjoys oneself so much — or a fool so little — as when being alone. In the Buddhist tradition, self love is a must. Many others may not know this, but individuals with Swagger do.

☞

The radio announcer with Super Swagger is one such as Howard Stern whose listeners are divided between half who love him and half who hate him. They all continue to listen to him, however.

The Book of Swagger puts Edmonton's CKUA radio station in the number 1 position in the *Top 10 Radio Stations in the World with the Most Swagger*. BBC Radio 2 didn't make the cut. Fact is, BBC Radio 2 would have a lot more Swagger if it played as much great blues music as CKUA's Holger Petersen does.

Workers with Swagger prize independence much more so than teamwork. The biggest problem with teamwork is that the people who bring the least — or absolutely nothing — to the table normally are the ones claiming all the credit when the project succeeds. As American aviation pioneer Igor Sikorsky reminded us, "The work of the individual still remains the spark that moves mankind ahead even more than teamwork."

೪

Individuals with Elegant Swagger are always better prepared for important situations than others think they should be for the same situations.

೪

The great Spanish artist Pablo Picasso once boasted, "I do not seek. I find." The same applies to super achievers with Swagger.

Not only as a sense of duty to humankind, but also to set an important example, it is the character with Swagger who eagerly dives into the water to save a drowning person when all others present won't take the risk.

An author with Super Swagger knows that a manuscript is never improved by showing it to friends and acquaintances and asking for advice before it is completed.

If an author with Super Swagger is asked to make a substantial change to a book, the author quips, "Who am I to tamper with a Masterpiece!"

Freedom of expression is the only law that Swagger recognizes.

Swagger is the power of expressing an individuality that is creative, resourceful, and productive. It's the creative people with Swagger throughout the ages — the ones willing to risk, think differently, challenge the status quo, and ruffle a few feathers — who have made the biggest difference in this world.

ॐ

Misery doesn't only love company. It demands it. For this reason individuals with Swagger don't only walk away from toxic people. They sprint!

ॐ

A lot of society can be downright savage to individuals with Swagger. These individuals do not worry because this same lot is savage to all successful and accomplished people.

Individuals with Swagger light their own fires instead of waiting around to be warmed by someone else's.

◌◌

For the achiever with Super Swagger, 3C Vision consisting of the three elements of critical thinking skills, creative thinking skills, and common sense is more important than a college education. It was for this reason that 16th Century French writer and philosopher Michel de Montaigne remarked, "I prefer the company of peasants because they have not been educated sufficiently to reason incorrectly."

◌◌

Individuals with Swagger know better than to sleep three in a bed, knowing full well that if they do, they will wake up three in a bed.

More often than not achievers with Swagger will face criticism, not because they are doing something wrong, but because they are doing something right. They don't get too bothered, however. As an unknown wise person pointed out, "A tiger doesn't lose sleep over the opinion of sheep."

∞

People with Swagger are spontaneous on a regular basis. "The less of routine, the more of life," observed A. B. Alcott.

∞

When Leonardo da Vinci was asked what was his greatest accomplishment in life, he replied, "Leonardo da Vinci." In this regard, achievers with Swagger don't try to be something or someone they aren't. They become more truly and more fully who they truly are.

"Individuality of expression," stated Johann Wolfgang von Goethe, "is the beginning and end of all art." The same applies for Swagger as much as it does for art.

ଔ

In the same realm, Oscar Wilde proclaimed, "Art is the most intense mode of individualism that the world has known." Of course, Swagger is a close second.

ଔ

At least once a year, the industrious worker with Swagger takes the boss to lunch or dinner — and doesn't cheap out!

ଔ

The individual with Elegant Swagger always asks the cashier at a checkout line how she is doing that day.

Achievers with Elegant Swagger don't waste energy and precious time arguing with unreasonable people. They realize that there is insanity on both sides of the issue when they catch themselves doing this.

❧

In a modern business marketplace in which only the quick and agile survive, super achievers with Swagger know that the boldest plans are often the safest.

❧

Happiness has many forms. Super achievers with Swagger attain high-octane happiness through self-esteem, action, achievement, success, prosperity, gratitude, solitude, and real friendship.

All people can be put into two categories; those with Swagger and those without. The character with Raunchy Swagger has only a vague curiosity about the latter.

Super achievers with Swagger never embrace what they don't want. They know that if they do, they are liable to get it.

Financial Swagger is realizing you are not as good as you should be at investing in dividend stocks and instead turning over your entire retirement portfolio to a financial advisor who gets you an annual average return of 9 percent after deducting the fees.

To avoid the staying power of mass delusion, achievers with Swagger don't hang around crowds all that much.

Many international airlines have Swagger for various great reasons. One of the many reasons Air Canada has Swagger is that the pilots of its Dreamliners have a habit of inviting the author of this book for a chat in the cockpit once the plane lands at its destination.

When deplaning, individuals with Elegant Swagger always smile and thank the flight attendants and the pilots for the safe and pleasant flight.

രജ

Many in society dwell in despair and believe in conspiracy theories as the cause of their low position in life. People with Swagger dwell in possibility and opportunity and don't believe in conspiracy theories. They actually find them very funny.

രജ

People with Swagger never use their teeth to open things.

രജ

When the woman with Elegant Swagger is a guest of someone else, she never complains about the food, drinks, or accommodations provided.

Achievers with Swagger answer their phones immediately when friends or business contacts call. If they are on the phone and can't respond, they do so immediately after ending the call even if the caller hasn't left a message.

∞

Financial Swagger is truly owning your own dream home with no mortgage or liens on it.

∞

Super achievers with Swagger roll the way they want to roll. There are limits, however. Integrity is a factor. They have respect for the law and for the rest of humanity.

∞

Super achievers with Swagger know that time spent enjoying themselves is never wasted.

If individuals with Super Swagger see a path clearly laid out step by step by others in society, they know that it's not their own path. Indeed, it can be a terribly wrong path.

☙

Achievers with Swagger don't feel that God burdened them with the work they have to do to make a good living; they feel that God blessed them with the work they have to do to make a good living.

☙

Some individuals with Super Swagger are so intelligent that they can speak on practically any subject. Most fools don't seem to need a subject.

An achiever with Super Swagger will never stay in a job that does not keep him or her fully and happily occupied.

☙

High achievers with Swagger are not afraid to start trends. "One thing is essential above all others — Swagger," claimed Dave McGinn of the *Globe and Mail*. He was referring to the "oh-so-epic" bat flip by José Bautista of the Toronto Blue Jays in 2015. At the time Bautista did it, this was considered arrogant and disrespectful by most players of all the other major baseball teams. Nowadays, the players of all the other major baseball teams happily flip their bats even more vigorously trying to be as cool as José Bautista was back then.

A super achiever with Swagger seldom listens to advice from the average person. Free advice is practically always overpriced. Put another way, talk is cheap because supply vastly exceeds demand.

◌

Super achievers with Swagger are prepared to grind it out. They know that going the extra mile or hanging on just one second longer than the competition is what leads to extraordinary success or being the winner in a crowded field.

◌

The train with Swagger keeps on its tracks. As the legendary motivational speaker Zig Ziglar pointed out, "Everybody says they want to be free. Take the train off the tracks and it's free — but it can't go anywhere."

Achievers with Swagger tend to ignore people who downplay or criticize any successful venture. As bestselling author and marketing guru Seth Godin wisely pointed out, "It's silly to try to delight the undelightable."

಄

Individuals with Elegant Swagger never keep a free ride waiting. Unlike freeloaders, they have a great deal of respect for anyone who is kind and generous enough to offer them the ride.

಄

Swagger, like art, flourishes when there is a sense of adventure.

಄

A lot of good arguments are spoiled by characters with Swagger who have great critical thinking skills and know what they are talking about.

162

Super achievers with Swagger love themselves totally. This is the Holly Grail of happiness.

Winning big without being able to show some Swagger is like eating in a five-star restaurant when you aren't the least bit hungry.

The person with Swagger doesn't mind being a minority of one.

Individuals with Swagger believe in being kind but they also realize it can be very costly being too kind. The more you give to certain people, the more they will demand from you. As Harvey Mackay warned, "If you want to be a Santa Claus, your sled better be able to pull a trailer."

People with Swagger experience freedom. "To be free," claimed Tennessee Williams, "is to have achieved your life."

α

Super Swagger is boasting to the sommelier in a 5-star restaurant that you know more about wine than the sommelier does — and then proving it!

α

Men and women of Swagger realize from experience that small minds are the first to criticize big ideas. Indeed, the narrower the mind, the wider the mouth. Put still another way, the emptier the wagon, the more noise it makes.

α

A moralist is an individual who falsely believes all individuals with Swagger are as evil as he is — and hates them for it.

It's okay for your child to have some Swagger. As the *Sunday Times* in London reassured us, "A youngster with a bit of Swagger is a real ray of light."

∝

Being unemployed will not deflate the ego of achievers with Swagger. They understand that being unemployed can be the true test of who they really are.

∝

Individuals with Swagger are adventurous in spirit and action, much more so than the mediocre people in society. As Jim Rohn stated, "If you are not willing to risk the unusual, you will have to settle for the ordinary."

∝

Characters with Swagger are boat rockers and not boot lickers.

A fool wanders aimlessly; the individual with Swagger travels intelligently.

ଔ

Entrepreneurial souls with Swagger are never hindered from starting a business because of the lack of funds. "Empty pockets never held anyone back," advised inspirational American cleric Norman Vincent Peale. "Only empty heads and empty hearts can do that."

ଔ

The individual with Swagger does not aid a good friend in trouble with mere advice; he or she gives the friend a big helping hand.

ଔ

The Doctor with Super Swagger is the one who has the author of this book as his or her patient.

Achievers with Swagger don't advertise their problems and troubles to friends and co-workers.

⚜

When critics speak evil of the achiever with Swagger, the achiever lives so that no decent, intelligent person will believe them.

⚜

To individuals with Swagger, being kind to themselves is just as important as being kind to others. They constantly remind themselves of their own great qualities that have created the great life that they have.

⚜

People with Swagger know that if they wait until retirement to really start living, they will have waited much too long.

When individuals with Elegant Swagger want to genuinely thank someone for something special, they don't text or email the person. They send a card with a nice handwritten note on the card. Alternatively, they phone the person to express their sincere gratitude.

଼

Individuals with Swagger have often not been great scholars nor have great scholars often been individuals with Swagger.

଼

Super achievers with Swagger understand that anyone with a bit of intelligence can achieve something important and make a big difference in this world. Contrary to popular belief, the key is not hard work, but finding the right thing to achieve.

Super achievers with Swagger keep going long after they think they can't.

❧

Individuals with Swagger dwell in possibility. As New Thought Movement author Thomas Troward so wisely reminded us, "The law of floatation was not discovered by contemplating the sinking of things."

❧

If the grass on the other side of the fence appears greener, achievers with Swagger don't climb over; they water their side.

❧

Super achievers with Swagger never imagine being successful in a short period of time. They know that overnight success only happens in fairy tales, trashy novels, and bad movies.

The price of Swagger, as for greatness, is responsibility and well-intentioned action. It's a continual learning experience.

ଔ

To the achiever with Swagger, one loss doesn't make a season. Neither do two or three in a row.

ଔ

The individual with Swagger hopes for the best but is always prepared for the worst. No one can live on hope alone but no one can live without it either.

ଔ

The creative individual with Swagger gets remarkable things done in a committee of three when the other two don't show up.

Successful people with Swagger believe in luck, but not in the same way as the majority in society do. As the late Super Swagger TV talk show host Larry King said, "You make your own luck. Luck is the residue of design."

∞

If you reach for the piano stool when helping others move a piano, you display no Swagger. Slothfulness, yes — but Swagger, no!

∞

Nice people are often not good people and good people are often not nice people. Because most individuals with Swagger are good people, they are often not nice people. In the same realm, these same individuals, because of their wisdom, have learned to never trust the nice person who speaks well of every one.

The individual with Swagger who has big dreams that he or she backs with constructive action is much more powerful than the person who claims to have all the facts and does nothing.

ॐ

Ordinary individuals stumble over pebbles; extraordinary individuals with Swagger stumble over mountains.

ॐ

Super achievers with Swagger see not only opportunities; they seize opportunities before anyone else has spotted them.

ॐ

Most in society will never understand the mindset of the super achiever with Swagger because they have never been super-good at anything.

In general, achievers are known by the company they keep. Achievers with Swagger are also known by the company they deliberately and fiercely avoid.

ଔ

Leaders with Super Swagger don't schedule $1,000 meetings to solve a $50 problem.

ଔ

Anyone with Swagger knows that more comfort doesn't necessarily mean more happiness. Comfort is a double-edged sword. A little will increase health and happiness. Too much, and it will destroy both.

ଔ

Even when they have major pains themselves, individuals with Elegant Swagger are not a pain to others.

173

Financial Swagger is having a butler.

Super achievers with Swagger when looking for more success in their lives reflect on where their previous success came from. It's no accident. Where their past success came from is where they put their future focus on.

Individuals with Swagger know that they have been truly successful when former classmates joyfully brag that they sat beside them in high school.

Older individuals with Swagger in their 70s, 80s, and 90s still focus on their dreams and not on envy and regret like a lot of people their age do.

The older achiever with athletic Swagger is one who at 73 years of age, after having enjoyed half a bottle of wine, can kick nine inches above his head with either foot without first warming up.

Super achievers with Swagger work to make their goals reality with unwavering confidence and practicing the master-of-your-own-destiny commitment that the majority in society know nothing about.

☙

To have more Swagger, fill your life with fulfilling experiences — and not excuses — that you can share with others.

☙

If there are 20 people in a hayloft, the character with Raunchy Swagger will be first to jump off.

☙

An individual with Super Swagger will wear a Mickey Mouse watch with the same flair as a Rolex or an Apple watch.

A long leisurely vacation, to super achievers with Swagger, is best enjoyed when they have truly earned it.

Individuals with remarkable insight and integrity respect the successful Swagger person's accomplishments for their merit; the rest of the public attribute the accomplishments to luck.

Super achievers with Swagger take 100 percent responsibility for their lives while being their own hero, becoming truly prosperous and free, without the sanction of society, government, friends, family, or any other forces that have no idea what a lifestyle of Swagger is all about.

Super Achievers with Swagger do not have mid-life crises.

Achievers with Swagger are not stingy with their friends and acquaintances. They know that generosity will always leave a more pleasant memory than stinginess.

⊂⊃

The duty of a leader with Swagger is to transform weakness into strength, problems into opportunities, obstacles into stepping stones, and disaster into superb accomplishment.

⊂⊃

Super achievers with Swagger think for themselves and always question convention and authority — just like Albert Einstein did. They, nonetheless, will acknowledge the wisdom of convention and authority and follow it when it is appropriate for the betterment of humanity. Just like Einstein did!

High achievers with Swagger know that it's impossible to become a hero to others without taking major risks in life.

⅘

People with Swagger make the smallest moves that give them the biggest gains. That's what genius is all about. It's also known as working Swagger smart instead of working idiot hard.

⅘

The individual with Swagger shoots at something no one else sees — and hits it.

⅘

The top compliment an individual with Swagger will ever give to a friend or business associate is that the friend's or associate's word is as good as gold.

High achievers with Swagger know that every great idea started as a unique untried idea. The problem is that great new ideas are unfamiliar and are rejected by the majority. When Led Zeppelin first performed *Stairway to Heaven* live, the audience was bored to tears waiting for a song they knew. The audience wanted hits, not something new. Luckily, Led Zeppelin embraced their own Swagger and stuck with the song. The rest is history.

For the corporate leader with Swagger, leading by example is not the main thing in influencing others — it is the only thing.

The true measure of individuals with Swagger is the height of their standards, the breadth of their knowledge, the depth of their understanding, and the length of their perseverance.

Individuals with Elegant Swagger are generous with praise but cautious with promises.

∞

Most of the world dreams and talks of achieving worthy accomplishments while the achiever with Elegant Swagger actually dreams and attains these accomplishments without first talking about them.

∞

Achievers with Swagger never grow up. Youthfulness of spirit guides them in tandem with great optimism. They are forever young in spirit and spend their entire lives in the most inspirational, adventurous, and creative ways possible.

Happiness is a by-product of achievement. So is Swagger.

ೞ

There is only one sensational success for super achievers with Swagger — to be able to spend their lives in their own remarkable ways.

ೞ

Achievers with Swagger live their best and always do their best. The results that they attain are, in fact, excellent. Whatever the results, they couldn't have come out any better.

ೞ

Super achievers with Swagger are constantly learning. They live by the much quoted adage from *Life's Secret Handbook*: "Be a Learner first, a Master second, and a Student always."

To super achievers with Swagger, charity starts at home but it doesn't stop there. They give a lot more to charities than the average person does because they truly believe in the importance of making a big difference in this world.

Psychiatrists and psychologists don't make much money off super achievers with Swagger — no inferiority complexes!

Individuals with Elegant Swagger try to treat everyone they encounter with respect. At the same time, they demand respect from other people and will eliminate these people from their lives if they don't get this respect.

When individuals with Elegant Swagger are given free tickets to an event, they never complain about the performance.

ભ

Taking the extra effort that others won't is a Swagger move. It takes not that much extra effort to be considered outstanding. Going the extra mile puts you miles ahead of the competition.

ભ

Fortune smiles upon individuals with Swagger who can laugh at themselves.

ભ

Achievers with Swagger never fight a battle when there is nothing precious to win. Only fools do this.